This book belongs to

_____

_____

_____

THE DOODLE, DESIGN, & DRAW BOOK

FOR ILLINOIS VALLEY KIDS

OF ALL AGES

Hey.

Isn't the copyright supposed to go on that page over there? And the title on this page? Copyright left, title right. That's how the other books do it.

First Edition
December 2015

9 8 7 6 5 4 3 2 1 0
Blast-off

Huh.

Well, maybe this isn't like those other books.

No forks were left in the making of this book

Left Fork

Dedicated to all
Illinois Valley (Oregon) kids *

* and some who are not

HOW TO USE THIS BOOK

1. Do not talk about how to use this book.[1]
2. You DO NOT talk about how to use this book.[2]
3. Doodling will go on as long as it has to.
4. If this is your first IV doodle book,
   you have to draw.
5 There are no rules.[3]

Notes

1. Other than to talk about how to not talk about how to use this book, of course. Hmm. But talking about not talking is still talking. Unless it's all written down. So maybe just don't say this out loud?

2. We really mean it this time. In fact, we are (just about) done describing how to best use this book by not talking about how to use this book (which, by the way, is different from talking about how not to use it). Really, just do what you want. Doodle, draw, write manifestos, make paper airplanes, get your fire started, whatever.

3. Alright, this is really the point we're trying to make (see final sentences in Note #2 above). Though, yes, it is a bit contradictory whenever someone says the only rule is that there are no rules—I mean, isn't that a rule? But if this can be called a rule, then perhaps it is better classified as one of those so-called "rules that are meant to be broken." [4]

4. Wait—that doesn't make sense. If you break a rule that there are no rules, wouldn't that mean that there *are* rules? Can we just say this is the rule that breaks its own rule, and leave it at that? Okay, time to stop reading! Move along! Get your Doodle on. And doodle on...

CONGRATULATIONS!
You've finally made it to THE BEGINNING*

PERSONALIZE these pages
so that in case you lose this book,
there's NO WAY someone else can say it's theirs

*** Though maybe you *started* here
so perhaps it's not that big of a deal**

HAPPY NEW YEAR!
Make a resolution and forget auld acquaintances
(or something like that)

On these pages,
draw your RESOLUTIONS

PAGE MOUNTAIN SNOW PARK!
But where is all the snow?

Draw what COVERS the snow park this year

No limits

Just DRAW

Draw the cover of your favorite book
at the IV BRANCH of
JOSEPHINE COMMUNITY LIBRARIES

Then make up a new book!
Is it by YOU?

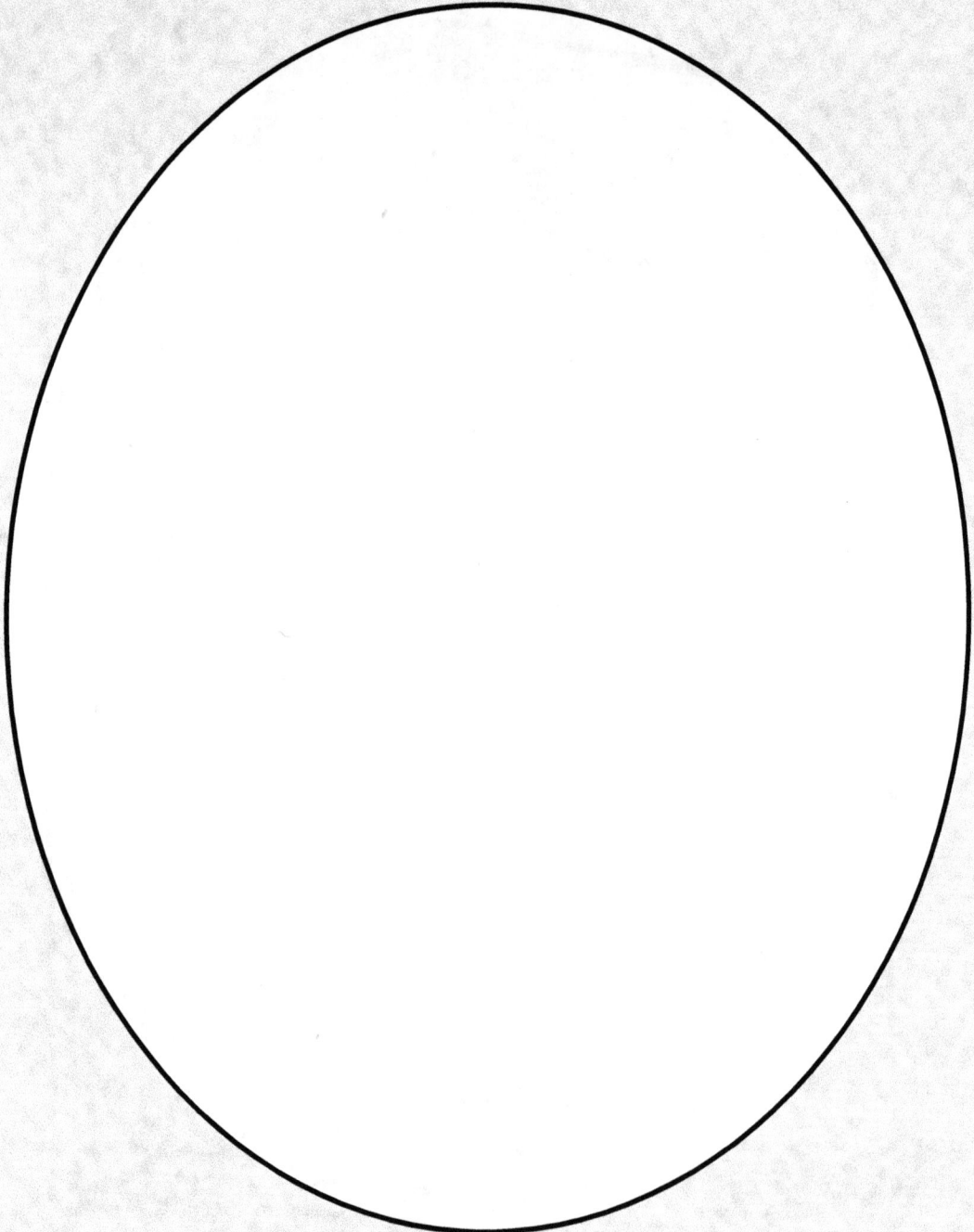

This page is for your
SELF-PORTRAIT

This page is for your self-portrait of
SOMEONE ELSE

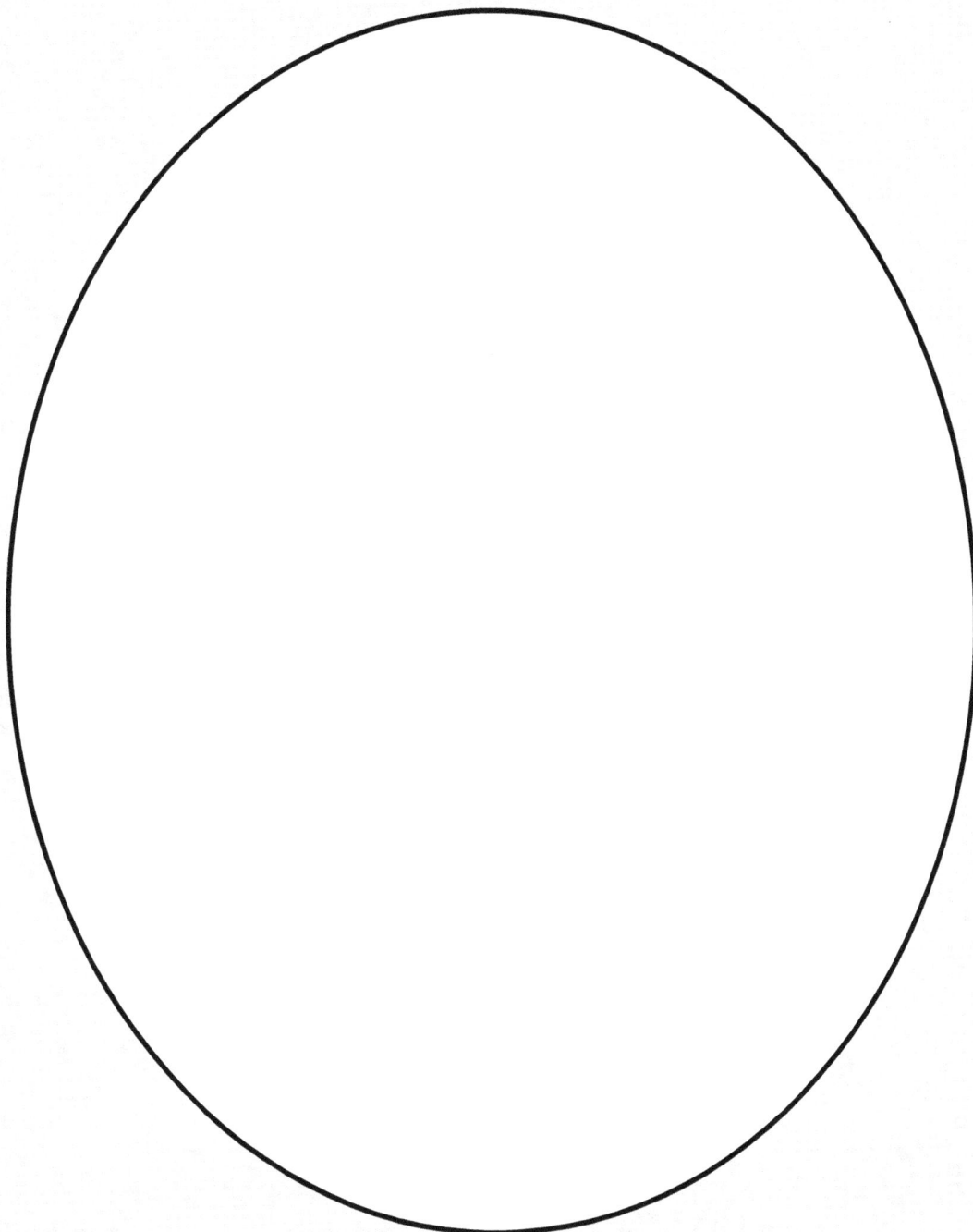

February has the fewest days
Draw something TINY but make it BIG

Now draw something usually
GINORMOUS
but make it EXTRA SMALL

Draw your favorite thing about WINTER in the ILLINOIS VALLEY

Draw your least favorite thing about WINTER in the ILLINOIS VALLEY

How much COLOR can you add to these pages?

You are hereby dared to make this the
PERFECT PIZZA

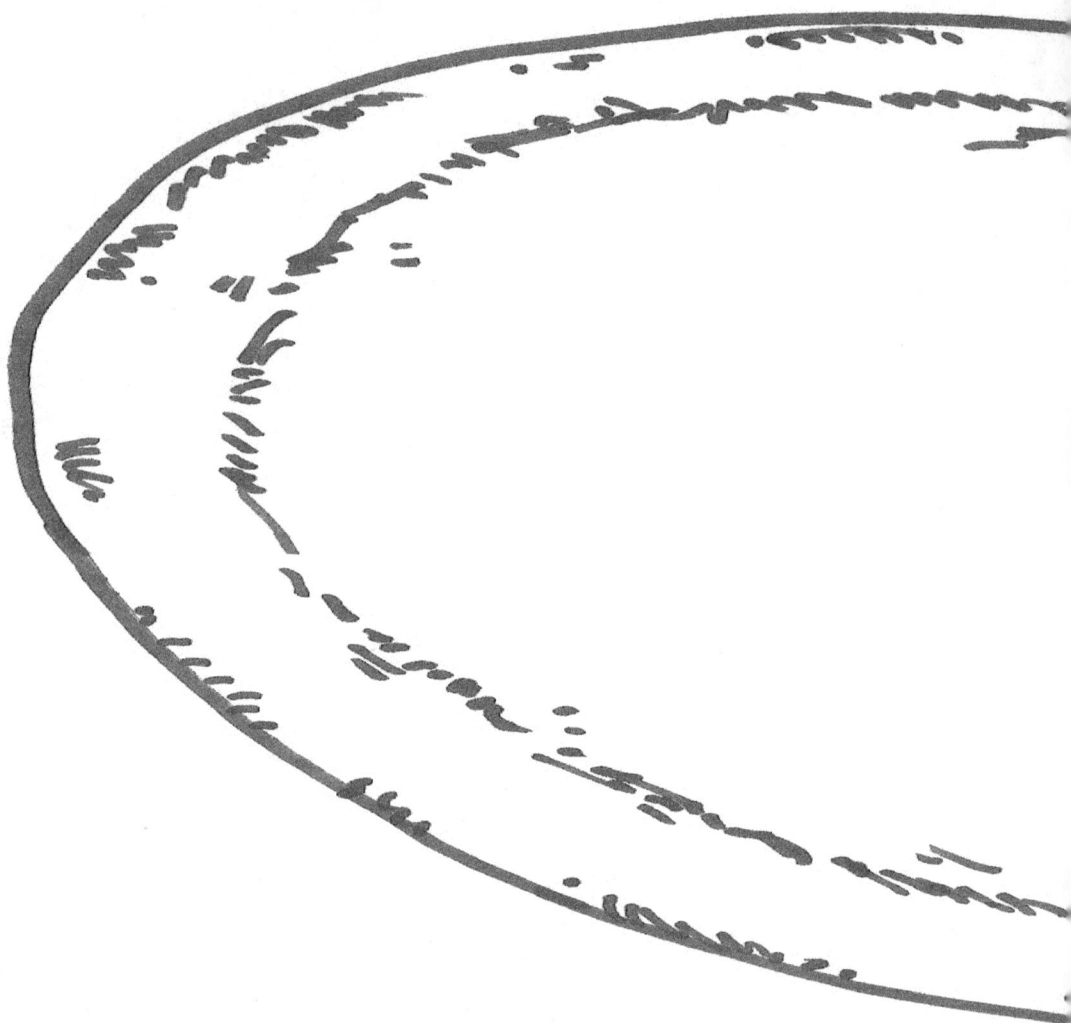

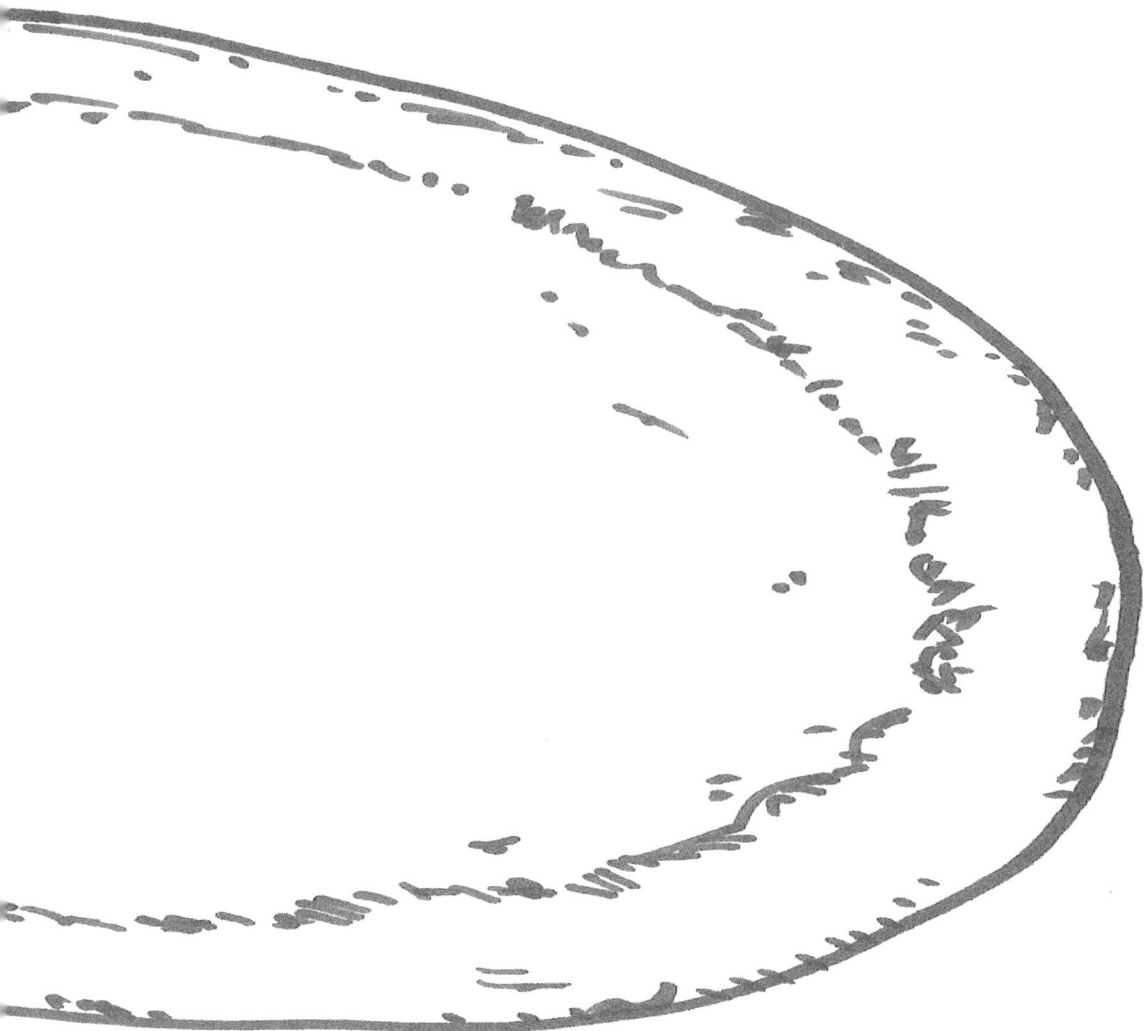

Draw a COBRA LILY at the
$8 MOUNTAIN BOARDWALK

Then submit your Cobra Lily to COBRA LILY*

Cobra Lily

a review of southwest oregon literature and art

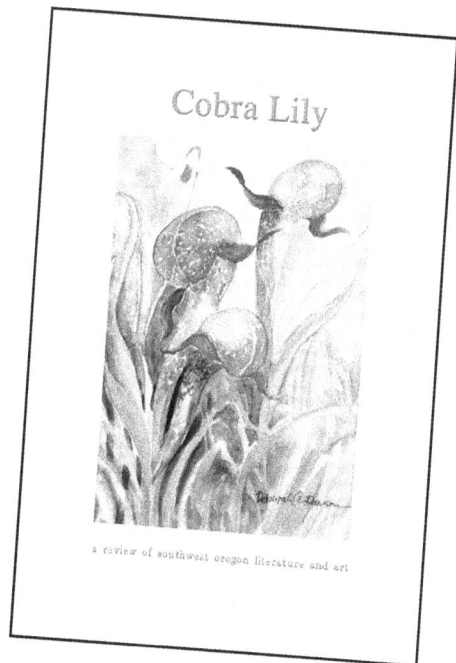

* You do know about COBRA LILY, right?
If not, get ye now to www.CobraLily.org!

Slow news week, so YOU get to choose
the headline, lead story, and photo
in THE ILLINOIS VALLEY NEWS

The Valley's #1 News S...

Illinois Val

Today, This Week, This Year

Since 1937

ey News

Published Weekly Cave Junction, Oregon 97523

MAR

Pick a color, any color

Now draw everything around you that is
YOUR COLOR

MAR

You discover a new species of wildflower
in bloom at ROUGH AND READY
Draw it!

Then name it!

APR

The CJ FARMERS MARKET is back!

What's growing in YOUR garden?

Color the cool ol' cop car at the O'BRIEN MARKET

(and yes, it's a cop car, but don't limit yourself to just black & white)

Draw a DREAM you had

APR

Community Day at the
OREGON CAVES NATIONAL MONUMENT

What do
YOU
discover
deep
down
underground?

MAY

MAY

Community Day at
GREAT CATS WORLD PARK

Can you draw the ROAR of the LION?
How about the GROWL of an OCELOT?

Now how many words can you make
from the letters in SIBERIAN TIGER?

We'll get you started...

- BITE
- RANT
- TAB

Draw your favorite thing about SPRING
in the ILLINOIS VALLEY

Draw your least favorite thing about SPRING in the ILLINOIS VALLEY

Check out the great condiment bar
TAYLOR'S SAUSAGE

Now go top your TAYLOR DOG!

SCHOOL'S OUT for summer!
But this is the I.V.
so school buses are ALWAYS in style

Color this one

There's space for new playground equipment at JUBILEE PARK

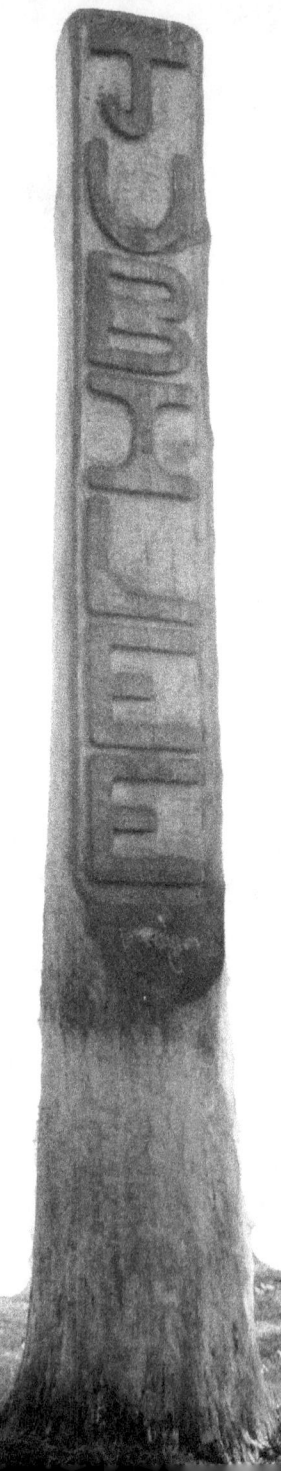

What do YOU design?

Join **HEALTHY U** at the
MOON TREE RUN & FIREFIGHTER'S FAIR
at the **SISKIYOU SMOKEJUMPER BASE**

Can you draw a FIREFIGHTER taking
a healthy stroll on the **MOON?**

JUN

Please design the next
HOPE MOUNTAIN
BARTER FAIRE!
t-shirt / poster thing

If you send it to them, you might win $100!
(No, really...tell 'em you read about it in this book)

Celebrate HATHKAPASUTA with us by coloring this SALMON

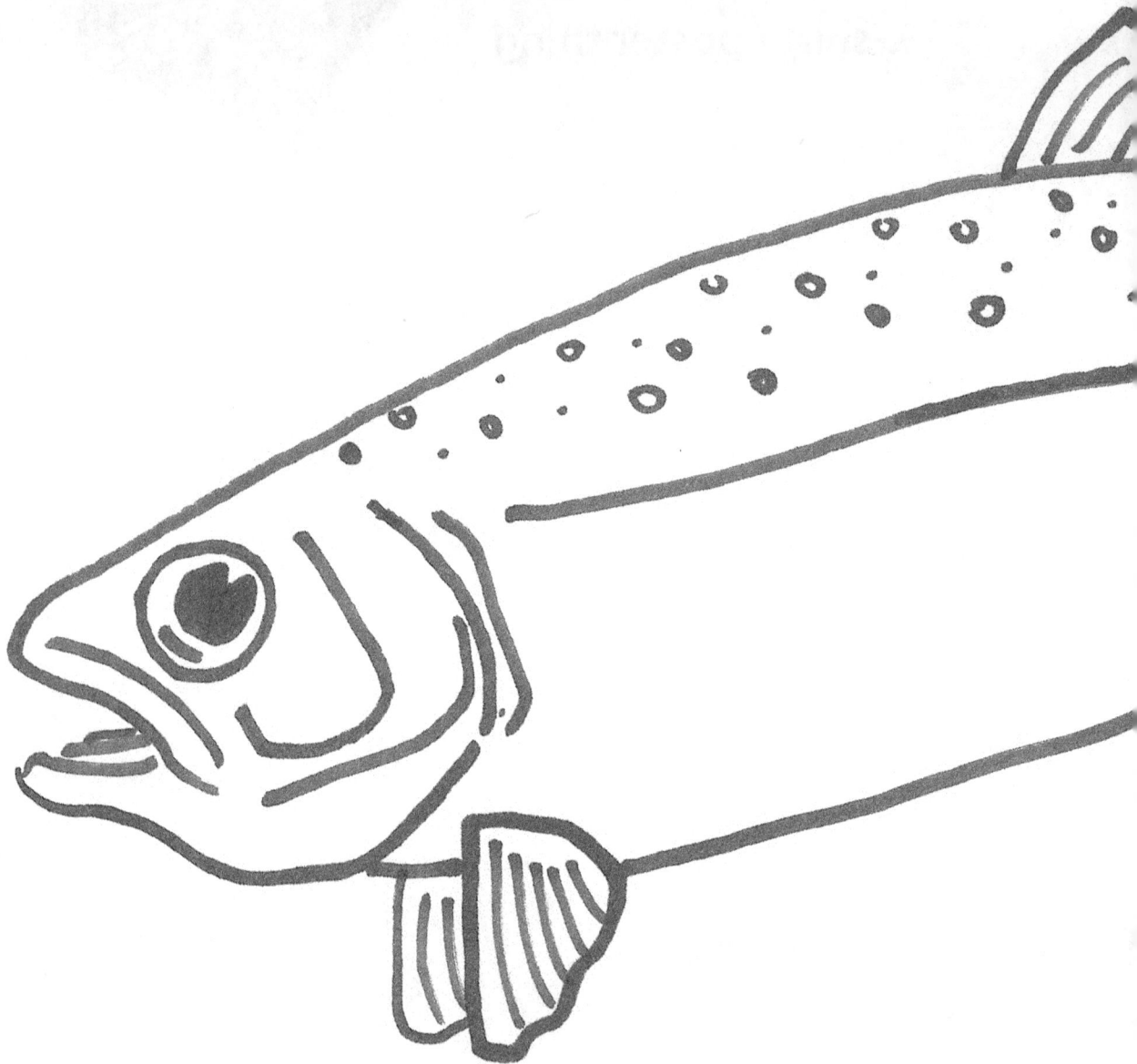

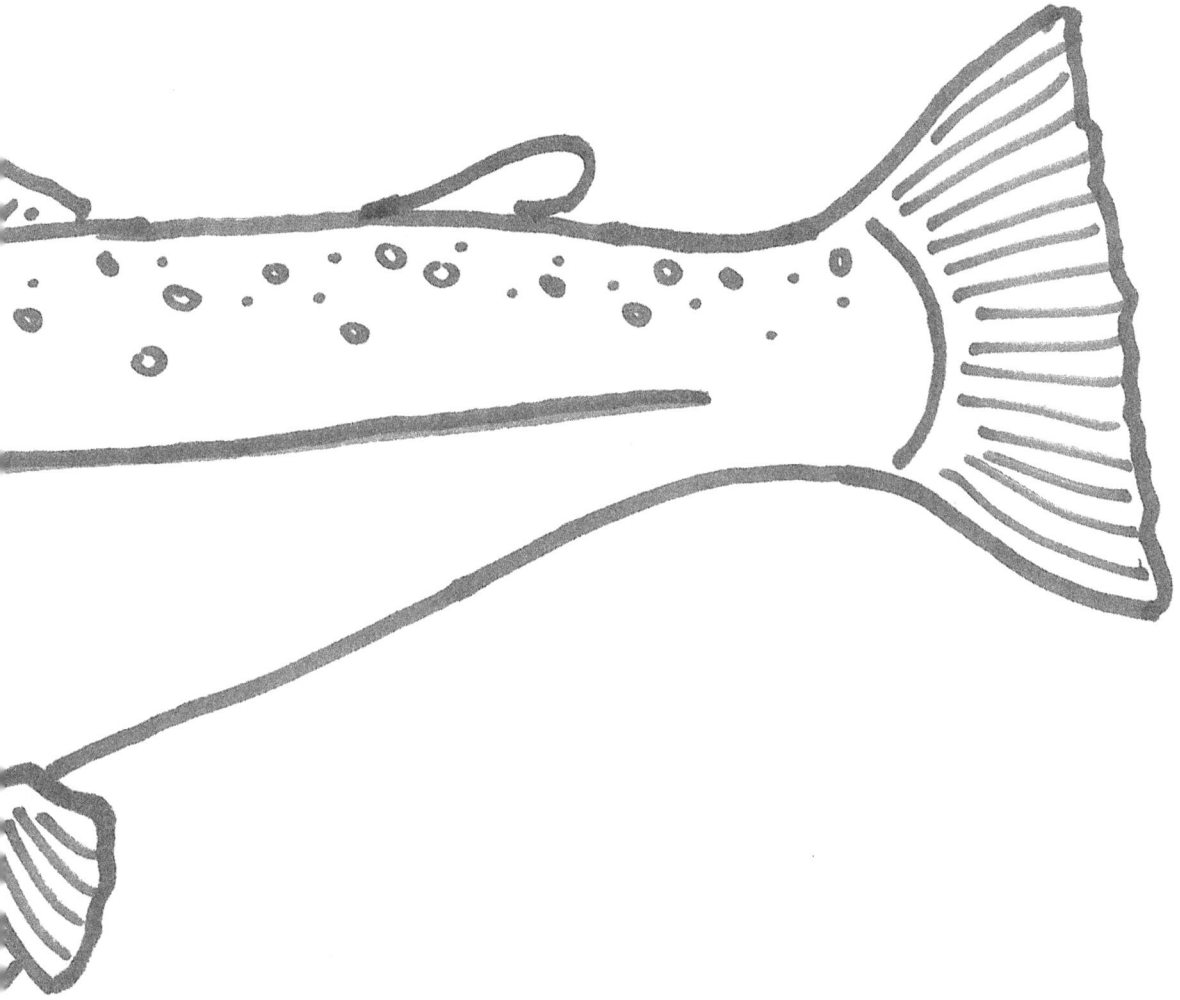

FREE SPACE

Draw whatever YOU want

**Better yet, draw something
you DON'T want to draw
(sometimes it's good to challenge yourself)**

Happy 4th of July!
Light up the night sky with some
FIREWORKS at OUT 'N' ABOUT

While you're here, go ahead and design their next TREEHOUSE*

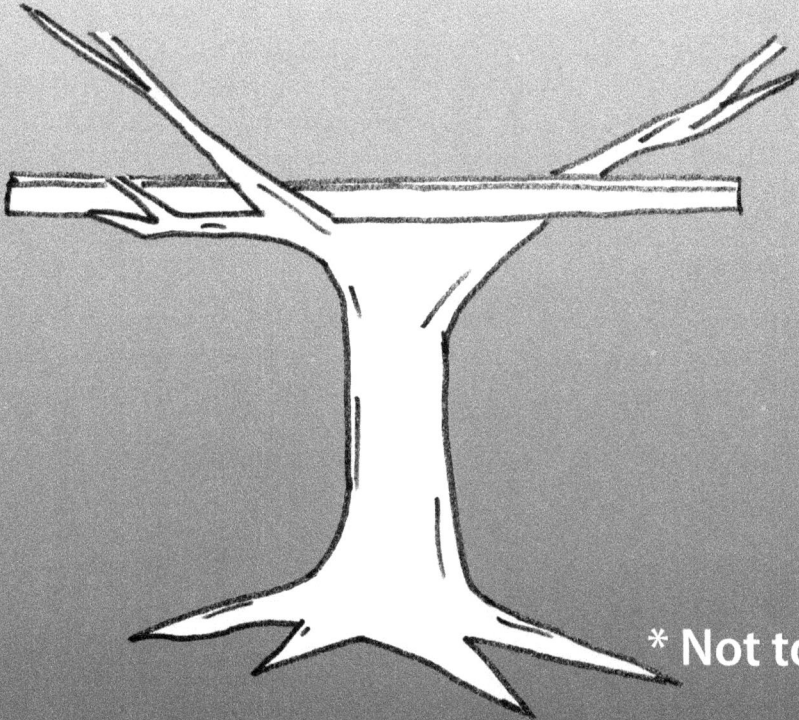

***Not to scale**

REUNION WEEKEND is here!

Let's revisit some IVHS math: If 74 people from 6 different classes (assume '78, '84, '89, '93, '02, and '11) show up to CARLOS RESTAURANTE all at the same time, how many spilled drinks will Kiki have to clean up by 9:26 pm?

Show your work*

* or maybe just draw an imaginary creature
eating at your favorite CJ restaurant

Color this butterfly
at the RUSK RANCH NATURE CENTER
BUTTERFLY PAVILION

Now draw your own
BUTTERFLIES

BLUEGRASS FEST!

Can you map the way from your house to the stage at LAKE SELMAC in time?

Is it the blackberries?
IT'S THE BLACKBERRIES!

Make an acrostic poem* from the word
BLACKBERRY

B

L

A

C

K

B

E

R

R

Y

* have the first letters of each line spell the word

Is it a burl?
IT'S A BURL!

Make an acrostic poem* from the phrase
IT'S A BURL

I

T

S

A

B

U

R

L

* for this poem, it doesn't need to be the *first* letters

Draw your favorite thing about SUMMER in the ILLINOIS VALLEY

Draw your least favorite thing about SUMMER in the ILLINOIS VALLEY

On these pages create your own
SECOND FRIDAY ART WALK
masterpieces*

* Need not be *visual* art: think of Michael Spring's
Art Walk masterpieces—his poetry!
What else could be an Art Walk masterpiece?

Nice day for a hike up
ONION MOUNTAIN

What do you see when you look out from the lookout?

Your float wins the prize at the IV Lions
LABOR DAY PARADE

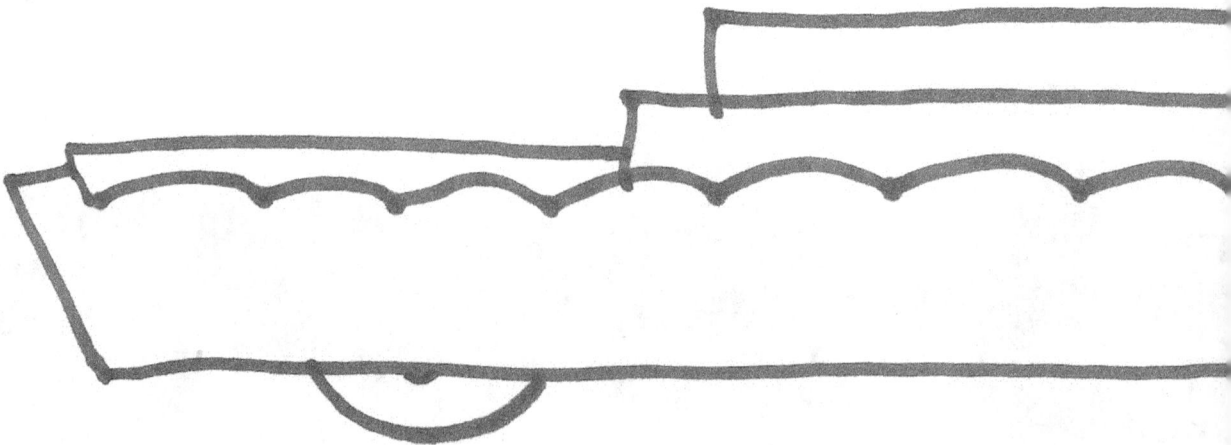

Here's what it looks like...
(we got you started)

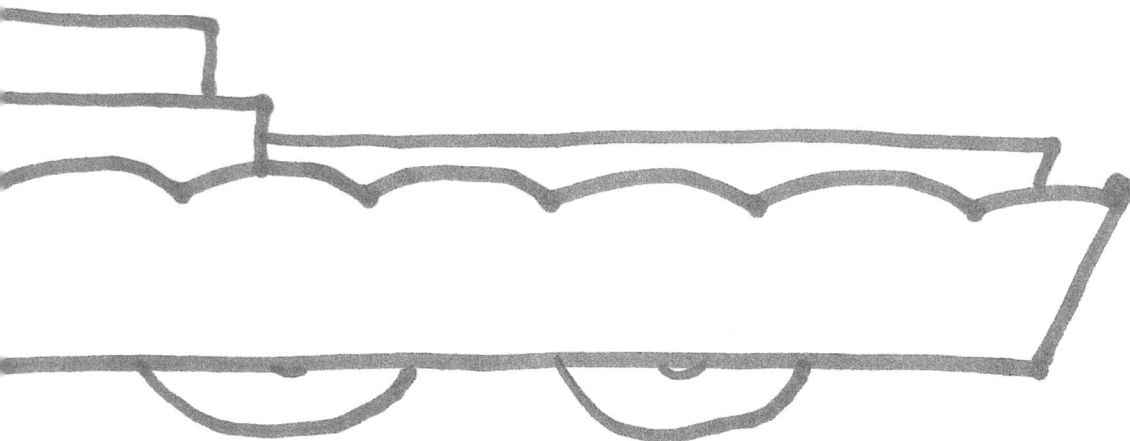

Back to school, already?

Your first assignment: fill these pages with what you did on your SUMMER VACATION

Killer SKATEBOARD, dude!

Show off the design on the bottom of your board

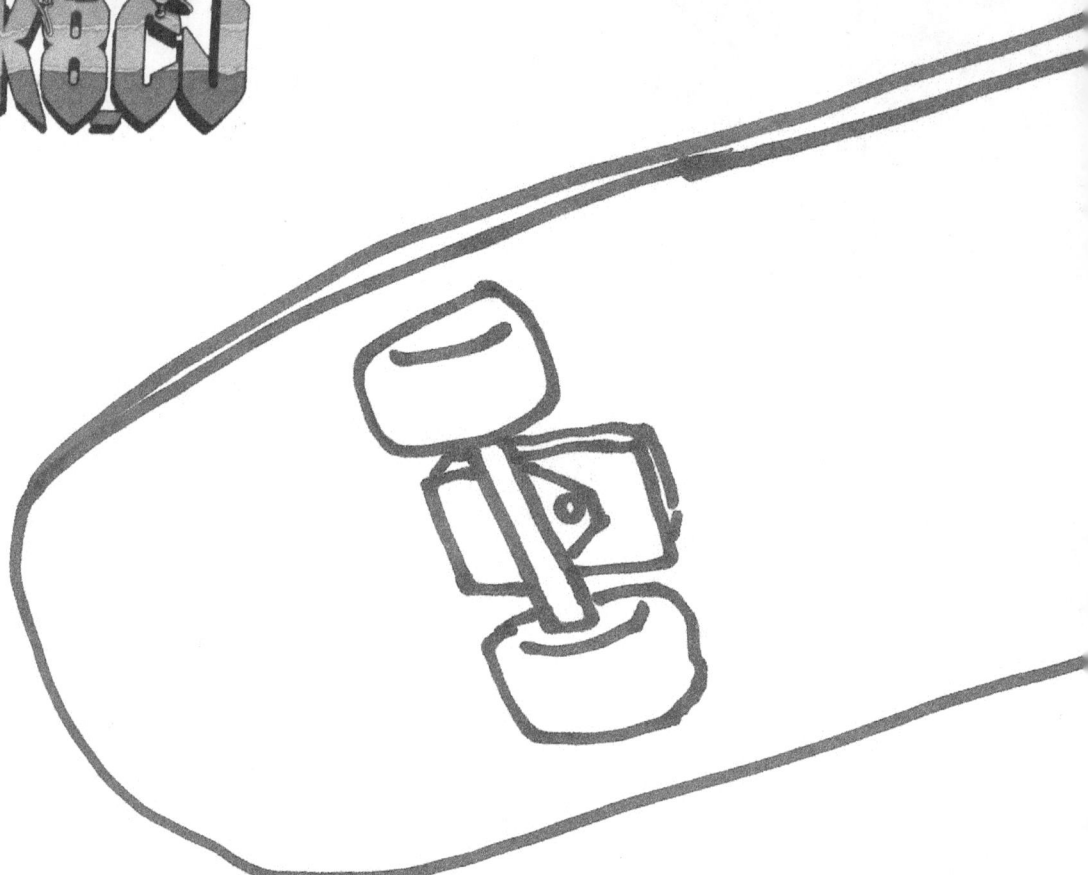

SK8CU

Draw an animal from the Illinois Valley in its NATURAL HABITAT

Your SCARECROW entry wins the $100 prize at the ACORN FESTIVAL!

What's the most interesting thing you can make with ACORNS?

These frames hold your masterpieces at the
SOUTHERN OREGON GUILD's
ARTOBERFEST

It's HALLOWEEN!

Carve your PUMPKIN

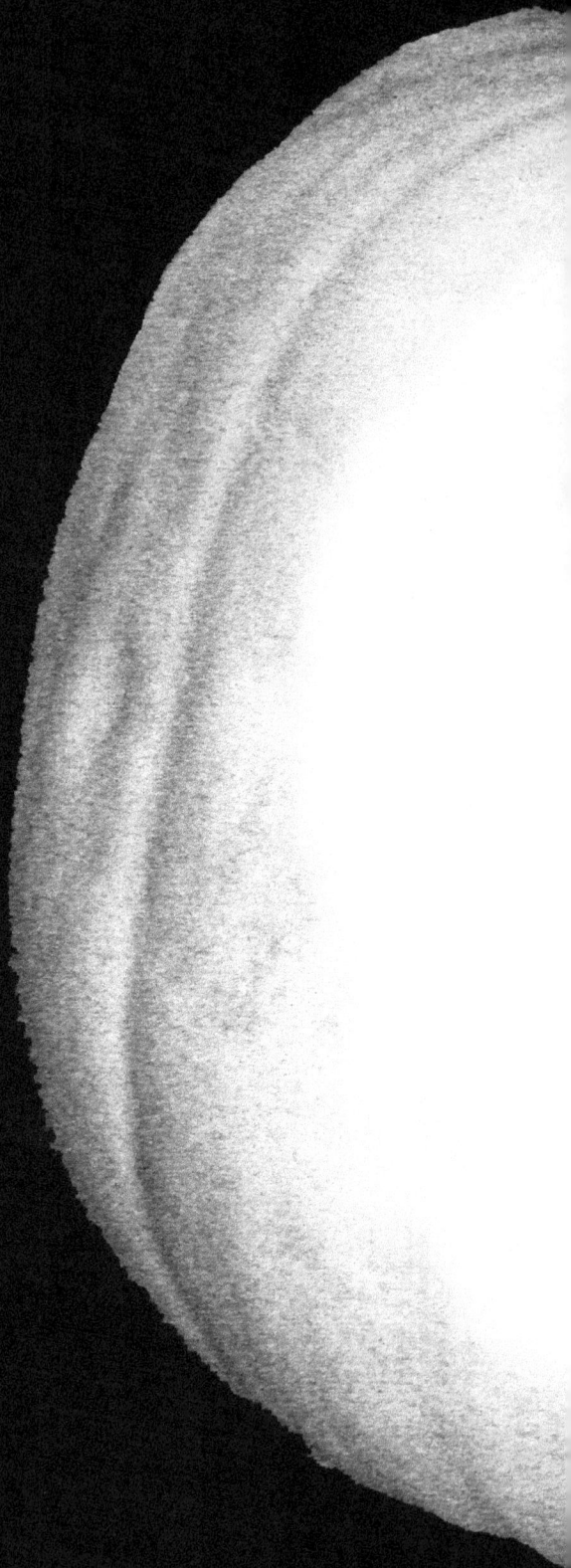

Time to Trick 'r Treat on HANBY LANE!
Design your COSTUME

Now draw a scary monster*
at IV HAUNT

* or not so scary

Draw your favorite thing about FALL
in the ILLINOIS VALLEY

Draw your least favorite thing about FALL in the ILLINOIS VALLEY

NOV

It's a DAY OF THE DEAD Celebration
at the DOME SCHOOL

Color your calacas!

**Then honor someone who has passed on
(could be a person but also a pet)
by drawing them here**

Without lifting your pencil
(or pen, crayon, marker, quill, finger, etc.),
draw an IMAGINARY CREATURE
at your favorite CJ restaurant

Wait—you did that for REUNION WEEKEND?
(and you think we're running out of ideas as we get near the end?? Ha! Try this...)

Then draw a REAL creature buying this very book
(and a coffee, and an Eggel on a white hiker)
at BAGEL JUNCTION

The **MUSHROOMS** are coming!
The **MUSHROOMS** are coming!

Fill these pages with all the
MUSHROOMS you can imagine

December means DANCEFARM dances, DELL'ARTE masks and melodrama making, and solstice SCROOGE stories
So write a play! *

Two characters are _____ & _____

Their conflict is _____

And the title is _____

Now it's YOUR turn...

*** Or just dance your crayon
around the stage page**

Don't think

Just DOODLE

Happy Christmas! Merry Hanukkah!
Seasons Solstice Diwali
Kwanzaa Greetings!

Draw your favorite HOLIDAY or HOLY DAY traditions here

Is it time for a VACATION?
Draw the view out your car window

**as you say goodbye to the ILLINOIS VALLEY
on your way to visit family in Ohio**

CONGRATULATIONS
You've made it to THE END*

As we used to ask at the end of interviews:
Was there something you were hoping to
share about yourself that we neglected
to ask you about?

* Even if you *started* here
(see notes about there being no rules),
this is a BIG DEAL!

About this book

No Illinois Valley businesses or locales paid for the inclusion of their name or likeness in this book. The selections were chosen by the designer and should *not* be construed as a *lack* of endorsement for any businesses *not* chosen. (Was that a triple-negative?)

If your business was named and for some reason you'd prefer to be removed from future editions, please contact us at leftforkbooks@gmail.com (and do accept our apologies).

If you're an Illinois Valley resident and have a suggestion for something that you feel should be included in future editions (you know, like SFI, Wild Rivers Pizza, etc.), please contact us at leftforkbooks@gmail.com. Thank you.

www.ingramcontent.com/pod-product-compliance
Lightning Source LLC
Chambersburg PA
CBHW080939030426
42339CB00009B/476